YEEHAW!

A Rootin' Tootin' Roundup of Country Positivity

summersdale

YEEHAW!

Copyright © Octopus Publishing Group Limited, 2024

All rights reserved.

Compiled by Saffron Hooton

No part of this book may be reproduced by any means, nor transmitted, nor translated into a machine language, without the written permission of the publishers.

Condition of Sale
This book is sold subject to the condition that it shall not, by way of trade or otherwise, be lent, resold, hired out or otherwise circulated in any form of binding or cover other than that in which it is published and without a similar condition including this condition being imposed on the subsequent purchaser.

An Hachette UK Company
www.hachette.co.uk

Summersdale Publishers
Part of Octopus Publishing Group Limited
Carmelite House
50 Victoria Embankment
LONDON
EC4Y 0DZ
UK

www.summersdale.com

Printed and bound in Poland

ISBN: 978-1-83799-588-2

This FSC® label means that materials used for the product have been responsibly sourced

MIX
Paper | Supporting responsible forestry
FSC® C018236

Substantial discounts on bulk quantities of Summersdale books are available to corporations, professional associations and other organizations. For details contact general enquiries: telephone: +44 (0) 1243 771107 or email: enquiries@summersdale.com.

To.........................

From....................

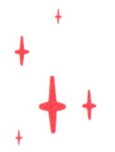

Every day is a new day, and you'll never be able to find happiness if you don't move on.

CARRIE UNDERWOOD

LIFE IS GETTING UP
ONE MORE TIME
THAN YOU'VE BEEN
KNOCKED DOWN.

John Wayne

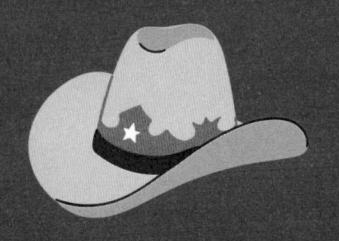

IF YOU SIT IN THE SADDLE, BE READY FOR THE RIDE

Big bug

An important person

There's an authenticity in just being who you are.

LUKE COMBS

BE
FEARLESS
AND
FREE

Speak your mind,
but ride a fast horse.

TEXAS BIX BENDER

Brisk up

To take a bold attitude

Put on your boots and face the day

Go where you're lookin', and look where you're goin'.

CLINT EASTWOOD

You're allowed to change and grow and be different.

MORGAN WADE

A GOOD HAT GETS BETTER AS IT GETS OLDER

Peace is a conscious choice.

JOHN DENVER

Cap the climax

To beat all and surpass everything

The great cowboys are the ones with the biggest hearts.

TY MURRAY

I WANT OPEN FIELDS, CRISP AIR, AND THE ROCKY MOUNTAINS AT THE END OF THE HORIZON.

Elsie Silver

RIDE AHEAD OF THE HERD

Catawampus

Something that is askew or awry

Storms make trees take deeper roots.

DOLLY PARTON

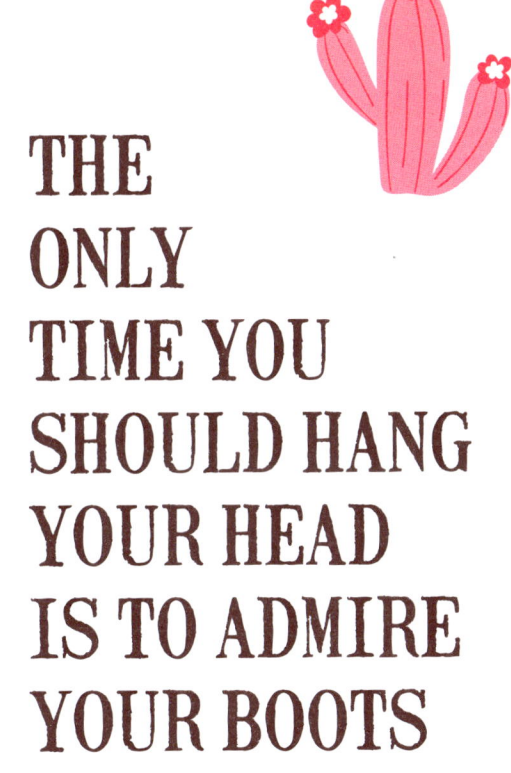

THE
ONLY
TIME YOU
SHOULD HANG
YOUR HEAD
IS TO ADMIRE
YOUR BOOTS

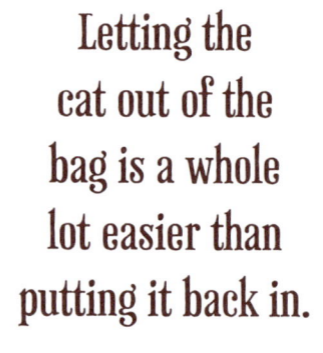

Letting the cat out of the bag is a whole lot easier than putting it back in.

WILL ROGERS

Cuter than a speckled pup in a red wagon

Adorable

Boot scoot to the beat of your own drum

I don't spend time wondering what might be next; I just focus on trying to savour every day.

TRISHA YEARWOOD

*For one to fly,
one needs only to
take the reins.*

MELISSA JAMES

THERE'S NOTHING SMALL-TOWN ABOUT YOUR AMBITION

Country music
is three chords
and the truth.

HARLAN HOWARD

Daisy

Good or excellent

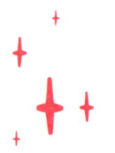

It's important to give it all you have while you have the chance.

SHANIA TWAIN

GO AFTER
THE DOORS
THAT ARE
OPEN TO YOU.

Chris Stapleton

LIFE LOOKS BETTER FROM UNDER A COWBOY HAT

Fair to middlin'

Feeling pretty good

Call me old-school but I think it's less about luck and chance and more about rollin' up your sleeves and showing up.

HAILEY WHITTERS

YOU
HAVE
THE
REINS

I never had a
compass in my life.
I was never lost.

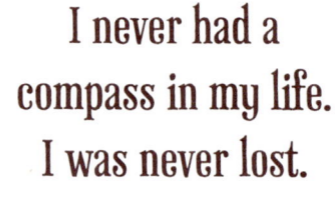

CHARLES GOODNIGHT

Fine as cream gravy

Very good

Life is an adventure; you've got to go through it

The boldest
plan is the best
and safest.

WILD BILL HICKOK

Cowgirl is an attitude, really; a pioneer spirit, a special American brand of courage.

DALE EVANS

ACT LIKE THIS AIN'T YOUR FIRST RODEO

If you can't do it on horseback, it probably ain't worth doing.

MONTIE MONTANA

Finer than a frog's hair split four ways

Dandy

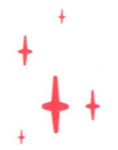

Life's up and down from the time you get here to the time you leave.

LUKE BRYAN

DESTINY IS THAT
WHICH WE ARE DRAWN
TOWARDS AND FATE
IS THAT WHICH
WE RUN INTO.

Wyatt Earp

VENTURING
OFF THE
BEATEN TRACK
OFTEN LEADS
SOMEWHERE
BEAUTIFUL

Fish or cut bait

Take action or stop saying that you will

*In the long run,
you make your own
luck – good, bad,
or indifferent.*

                                              LORETTA LYNN

TO
RIDE
A HORSE,
YOU'VE GOT
TO GET OFF
THE FENCE

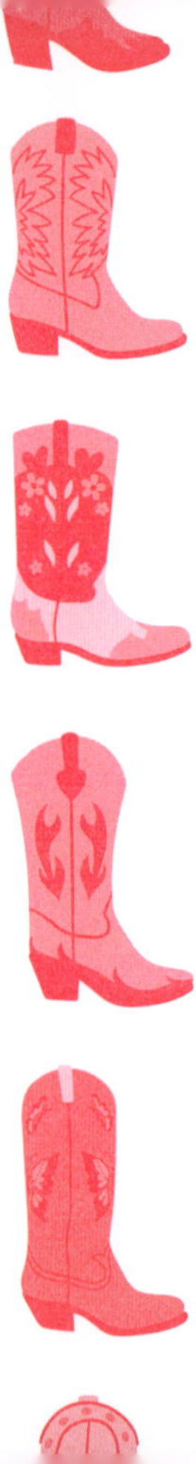

If you're gonna
be a dreamer,
you better be
a doer.

LAINEY WILSON

Happifyin'

Making happy

EVERY PATH HAS PUDDLES

What's
gonna happen,
gonna happen.

BILL PICKETT

> *Failing is part of the process. It's how you brush yourself off and get back in the saddle that counts the most.*
>
> — CARLY KADE

KEEP YOUR STANDARDS HORSE-HIGH AND YOUR DETERMINATION BULL-STRONG

Rodeo, like poetry, can get into your haemoglobin, into the deep helices of DNA, and once there it becomes your metaphorical makeup for life.

PAUL ZARZYSKI

Hoedown

A square dance

Grandpa Patterson used to say: Never approach a bull from the front, a horse from the rear or a fool from any direction.

DEBBIE MACOMBER

CONFLICT FOLLOWS WRONGDOING AS SURELY AS FLIES FOLLOW THE HERD.

Doc Holliday

SOME TRAILS
ARE BUMPY
BUT WE ALWAYS
LEARN FROM
THE RIDE

Head hog at the trough

A leader

Keep on aiming and keep on shooting, for only practice will make you perfect. Finally you'll hit the bull's-eye of success.

ANNIE OAKLEY

YOU MIGHT GET BIT, BOOTED AND BUCKED, BUT DON'T GIVE UP

No matter what happens in life, be good to people.

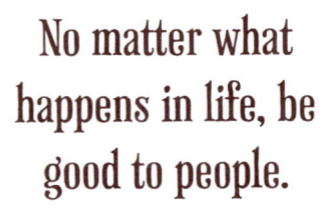

TAYLOR SWIFT

Hold your horses

Stay calm

No matter how bad your day is, remember there's always someone waiting for you at the barn

When I started
counting my blessings,
my whole life
turned around.

WILLIE NELSON

Inspiration is finding something that excites you.

CONNIE SMITH

EVERYBODY WANTS TO GROW UP AND BECOME A COWBOY

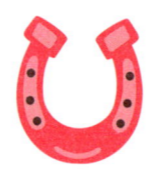

All your life, you will be faced with a choice. You can choose love or hate… I choose love.

JOHNNY CASH

Horse sense

Intelligence

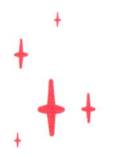

True country music is honesty, sincerity, and real life to the hilt.

GARTH BROOKS

I BELIEVE
YOU HAVE TO
LIVE THE
SONGS.

Tammy Wynette

BE ROOTIN',
BE TOOTIN',
AND HAVE A
GOOD TIME

Howdy!

A greeting

This is why you're here. This is what you are made to do. This is you.

TANNER ADELL

BORN
TO
RIDE

Scare off the people who are gonna be scared off, and then the right people will like you for who you really are.

KACEY MUSGRAVES

Huckleberry

The person for the job

Don't look back; you're not going that way

This is me.
Love it or leave it.

PRISCILLA BLOCK

I have an unending desire to be better and make myself a better person.

TANYA TUCKER

GO AFTER YOUR DREAMS LIKE THEY'RE THINGS THAT'VE GOT TO BE ROPED BEFORE THEY GET AWAY

**Take the risk,
bet on yourself.**

BRELAND

In apple-pie order

In top shape

The cowboy goes to the school of nature.

WILL JAMES

I COULD
NEVER RESIST
THE CALL OF
THE TRAIL.

Buffalo Bill

DON'T SELL YOUR SADDLE

It'll all come out in the wash

Everything will work out

Listen to advice, but follow your heart.

CONWAY TWITTY

RIDE OFF INTO THE SUNSET

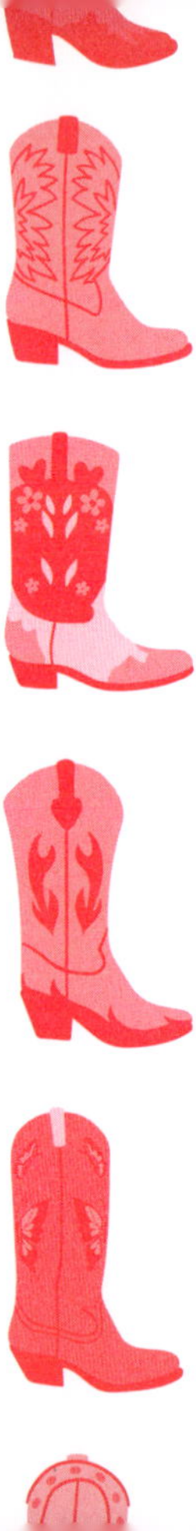

Life is just a
conglomerate of just
really random things
that sometimes
don't always piece
together, but
it's your life.

BRITTNEY SPENCER

Make a mash

To impress someone

Stay
wild

Be easy on your mind
today; what a good day
to be breathing in.

ZACH BRYAN

Put your hand on your horse and your heart in your hand.

PAT PARELLI

NEVER WALK WHEN YOU CAN RIDE

The greatest gift
I've been given is being
naive because I don't know
what I can't do. And when
you don't know what
you can't do, you think
you can do everything.

KELSEA BALLERINI

Of the first water

First class

If you're gonna sing, sing 'em something they can understand.

HANK WILLIAMS

> MUSIC IS UNIVERSAL; IT'S HEALING.
>
> *Crystal Gayle*

LIFE'S A
LONG JOURNEY
SO WEAR
COMFORTABLE
BOOTS

Pretty as a peach

Gorgeous

Nothing's so sacred as honour and nothing's so loyal as love.

WYATT EARP

BEING
A COWGIRL
AIN'T ABOUT
THE CLOTHES,
IT'S ABOUT
ATTITUDE
AND HEART

Life is all
about having a
good time.

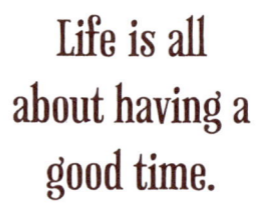

MILEY CYRUS

Right as a trivet

Stable

There's nothing that driving along country roads with the windows down can't fix

The key to change is
to let go of fear.

ROSANNE CASH

I've spent a lifetime in love with country music.

BLAKE SHELTON

BE KIND, LOYAL AND HONEST

I like being different...
As long as I know there's
a box, and I'm outside
of it, I'm good to go.

BRANTLEY GILBERT

Rootin' tootin'

Something that is exciting or impressive

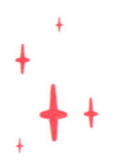

Each person has their own calling on this Earth.

BILLY RAY CYRUS

> YOU HAVE TO
> ACCEPT YOURSELF
> SO EVERYONE
> ELSE CAN.
>
> *Lauren Alaina*

COUNTRY MUSIC IS GOOD FOR THE SOUL

Sand

Guts or courage

I've always enjoyed things going at a nice pace, nothing too fast, nothing too crazy.

LUKE BRYAN

DON'T
FOLLOW
ANYBODY
ELSE'S
WAGON
TRACKS

It's about how resilient you are when failure faces you. The character that you hold, the values that you hold.

FALLON TAYLOR

Screamer

An extraordinary person

Always drink upstream from the herd

We all take different paths in life, but no matter where we go, we take a little of each other everywhere.

TIM McGRAW

Don't let anyone save you for later.

DASHA

LEAVE TUMBLEWEEDS TO THEMSELVES

There's no
blueprint for success,
and sometimes you just
have to work at it.

TAYLOR SWIFT

Someone to ride the river with

A reliable person

It was always very romantic to me: The West, the cowboy, the Western way of life.

REBA McENTIRE

FIND OUT WHO YOU ARE AND DO IT ON PURPOSE.

Dolly Parton

COUNTRY IS A WAY OF LIFE

Squinny

To laugh, wink or smile

Country music is the people's music.

FAITH HILL

SOMETIMES YOU'VE JUST GOT TO PUT ON YOUR BOOTS AND DANCE

If you find yourself in a hole, stop digging.

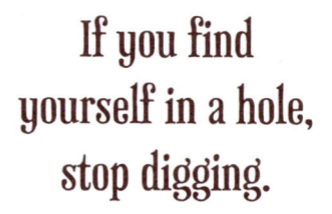

WILL ROGERS

Take the rag off the bush

To surpass

Don't squat with your spurs on

We all do stupid things; we're all just people.

OLIVER ANTHONY

Life unravels the way it does, and it has an effect on you, but you have to take responsibility for dealing with it.

SHANIA TWAIN

KEEP IT COUNTRY

When you open your mouth, have something new to say. Have your own style.

PAM TILLIS

Three-by-nine smile

A big smile

Courage is being scared to death and saddling up anyway.

JOHN WAYNE

DON'T EVER TRY AND
BE LIKE ANYBODY
ELSE AND DON'T
BE AFRAID TO
TAKE RISKS.

Waylon Jennings

YOU HAVE THE CHOICE TO FOLLOW THE TRAIL OR TO MAKE YOUR OWN PATH

Well, butter my butt and call me a biscuit!

An exclamation of surprise at something unbelievable

It's okay to feel in control one minute and out of control the next. We have to love ourselves fully and give ourselves grace to feel.

CARLY PEARCE

BE READY FOR THE RIDE

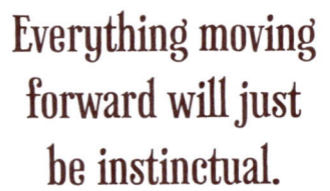

Everything moving forward will just be instinctual.

CODY JOHNSON

Winsome

Lively or cheerful

Everyone falls off their horse; don't quit the ride

You build on failure.
You use it as a
stepping stone.

JOHNNY CASH

Throw caution to the wind and just do it.

CARRIE UNDERWOOD

LIVE LIFE LIKE A COUNTRY SONG

I'm gonna be something one of these days.

PATSY CLINE

Yeehaw!

An exclamation of excitement

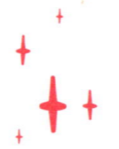

The Old West is not a certain place in a certain time; it's a state of mind. It's whatever you want it to be.

TOM MIX

I'M PRETTY SURE
I'M GONNA STICK WITH
COUNTRY UNTIL I RIDE
OFF IN THE SUNSET.

Darius Rucker

Have you enjoyed this book?
If so, find us on Facebook at
Summersdale Publishers, on Twitter/X at
@Summersdale and on Instagram and TikTok
at **@summersdalebooks** and get in touch.
We'd love to hear from you!

www.summersdale.com

Image credits

All illustrations © burbura/Shutterstock.com;
p.3 and throughout © Media Guru/Shutterstock.com